A New True Book

COMETS, ASTEROIDS, AND METEORS

By Dennis B. Fradin

CHILDRENS PRESS™

CHICAGO

1966 Leonid meteor shower photographed
from Kitt Peak National Observatory
near Tucson, Arizona. The brightest
star trail is Sirius, at left. The
constellation Orion is at right.
Can you see the meteor trails?

For Bernice Blaz

PHOTO CREDITS

Historical Pictures Service, Chicago—17

Dennis Milon/Sky & Telescope: 2, 31, 32, 35, 36, 38,
44 (2 photos); © George East—22

Finley Holiday Film—4, 19 (left), 25

NASA: National Aeronautics and Space
Administration—5, 8, 13, 21, 27

John Forsberg—6, 7, 40, 41

© 1963 AURA, Inc., Kitt Peak National Observatory,
19 (right)

© 1972 AURA, Inc., Kitt Peak National Observatory,
14 (top)

© 1973 AURA, Inc., Kitt Peak National Observatory,
14 (bottom)

© 1978 Lowell Observatory and AURA, Inc., Kitt Peak
National Observatory, 10

© 1979 AURA, Inc., Kitt Peak National Observatory,
15

Connecticut Department of Economic
Development—42

Meteor Crater Enterprises, Inc.—29

U.S. Naval Observatory—45

COVER—Halley's Comet

Library of Congress Cataloging in Publication Data

Fradin, Dennis B.
   Comets, asteroids and meteors.

   (A New true book)
   Includes index.
   Summary: Describes in simple terms the meteors,
comets, and asteroids that are part of our solar system
and discusses the various theories concerning their
origin and their effect on life on Earth.
   1.   Comets—Juvenile literature.   2.   Planets, Minor—
Juvenile literature.   3.   Meteors—Juvenile literature.
[1.   Comets.   2.   Planets, Minor.   3.   Meteors.   4.   Solar
system]   I.   Title.
QB721.5.F7   1984   523.2   83-23231
ISBN 0-516-01723-3

TABLE OF CONTENTS

THE SOLAR SYSTEM

A star is a ball of hot glowing gas. There are many trillions of stars. Space has more stars than a sandbox has grains of sand.

Close-up of our sun which is a burning star

One star is special to us. It is the closest one to us. Because it's so close, it gives us heat and light. This special star is the sun.

Many objects orbit (go
around) the sun. The sun
plus all objects that orbit it
are called the solar
system. Of all the objects
in the solar system, the
sun is by far the biggest.

The main objects that
orbit the sun are the
planets. There are nine

known planets. They are
Mercury, Venus, Earth,
Mars, Jupiter, Saturn,
Uranus, Neptune, and Pluto.
Most of the planets have
moons. Earth has one
moon. Jupiter has sixteen
moons. The moons are
part of the solar system,
too.

Spacecraft have photographed six of the planets in the solar system. In this composite picture the moon's surface is in the foreground, then the Earth, Venus (at left), Jupiter (far upper left), Mercury (second from left), Saturn (upper right), and Mars (center of photo).

The solar system has three other kinds of objects besides the sun, the planets, and the moons. The three are comets, asteroids, and meteors.

COMETS

In spring of 1910 Halley's Comet appeared. It was as bright as a bright star and it stretched halfway across the sky. People watched the comet for many nights. Finally it headed deep into space, not to return until 1986. Halley's Comet is the most famous comet. There are many other less-famous ones.

A computer, using a photo taken in 1910 at Lowell Observatory, put together this color image of Halley's Comet.

Astronomers call comets "dirty ice balls." That is because a comet's main part—the head—is a ball of ice with dust, metal, gases, and rock frozen inside.

When a comet nears the sun, the heat melts some of the ice. Dust and gases are released from the head. The dust and gases fan out. They become the tail of the comet. Comets' tails are millions of miles long. They always point away from the sun. That is because the sun creates a wind—the solar wind—that blows against the tail.

Each comet takes a certain time to orbit the sun. Halley's Comet takes about 76 years. Encke's Comet comes back every 3.3 years. Other comets take thousands or even millions of years to go around the sun. Only when a comet nears the sun can

In 1974 the Comet Kohoutek streaked through our solar system.

we see it with our eyes or
with small telescopes. That
is because the sun lights
up comets, just as it lights
other objects in the solar
system.

Observation room of
the solar telescope
(above) and the
exterior of the 4-meter
telescope at the
Kitt Peak National
Observatory

14

Astronomer adjusts controls on a telescope.

More than two thousand comets are known. Thousands are yet to be discovered. Comets that appear every few thousand years or longer await discovery because no one recorded their past visits. Many astronomers spend their nights looking through telescopes for comets.

There have been many

famous comet hunters. The Frenchman Jean Louis Pons (1761-1831) found the most comets—thirty-seven. The American Edward Emerson Barnard (1857-1923) found twenty-two. An English woman, Caroline Herschel (1750-1848), found eight. Comets are named for their discoverers. The Comet Ikeya of 1963 was discovered by nineteen-year-old Kaoru Ikeya of Japan.

Edmund Halley was an English astronomer.

No one knows who discovered Halley's Comet. It has been seen every seventy-six years or so for more than two thousand years. It was named for Edmund Halley (1656-1742).

He was the first to realize that comets orbit the sun and that they come back again and again.

Where do comets come from? It is thought they were formed at the solar system's outer edges when the solar system began. How this happened is not known. Several countries are sending spacecraft to study Halley's Comet on its 1986 return. Perhaps we will then learn more about the origin of comets.

ASTEROIDS

   On January 1, 1801, the
Italian astronomer
Giuseppi Piazzi was
looking through his
telescope. He saw a small
unknown object between
·the planets Mars and
Jupiter.

Left: Mars
Below: Jupiter

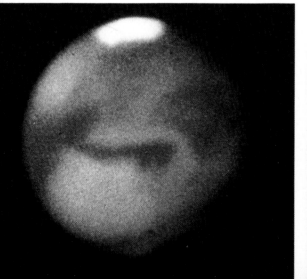

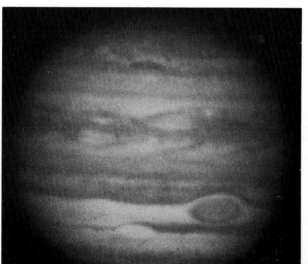

Later other astronomers found many more small objects between Mars and Jupiter. These objects, made of rock and metal, are called asteroids. About two thousand asteroids have been observed. Astronomers think there are many thousands more.

The asteroid discovered by Piazzi is named Ceres. Although just 485 miles in diameter, Ceres is the biggest asteroid. Pallas, Juno, and Vesta are the

Artist's drawing shows solar-powered system of the future. Spacecraft, such as the space shuttle, might retrieve asteroids for industrial use.

three other largest ones. Most asteroids are just a few miles or less in diameter. Many are no bigger than a hill and have odd shapes. A few asteroids have orbits that

Trail of Asteroid Eros

take them near our Earth.
In 1937 the tiny asteroid
Hermes came within a half
million miles of Earth.

As is the case with
comets, it is thought that

asteroids were formed at the birth of the solar system. Again, how this happened is unknown. According to one theory, the planets were formed from bits of dust and rock that came together. The asteroids are the pieces that failed to come together to form a planet.

METEORS

Only rarely is a comet visible to the naked eye. To view an asteroid, you need a telescope. But you can go out on most clear nights and see a meteor or two. Meteors appear as streaks of light flashing across the sky. Many people call them "shooting stars" or "falling stars," but meteors aren't stars at all.

They begin as pieces of rock and metal floating

A meteoroid shoots through the Milky Way.

through space. There are
billions of these bits of
material in the solar
system. When they are out
in space they are called
meteoroids.

As our Earth orbits the sun, every day it crosses the paths of some meteoroids. When a meteoroid comes into contact with Earth's air, it burns up. Meteoroids that burn up in the air are called meteors.

Most of the meteors we see streaking across the sky are about the size of a grain of sand. They burn up completely at a height of about fifty miles above the ground.

ALHA81005, 0

1 cm

Close-up of a meteorite found in Antarctica. Scientists found that this meteorite has characteristics very similar to moon rocks.

Now and then Earth crosses the path of a meteoroid the size of a golf ball, a basketball, or even a car. When this happens there may be a very bright meteor called a fireball. There may be a

loud roar as the fireball
passes over. Sometimes
the fireball explodes.

Pieces of fireballs
sometimes hit the ground.
A meteoroid that hits the
ground is called a
meteorite. There are two
types of meteorites—stony
and iron.

Once in a great while a
huge meteorite strikes
Earth. In Arizona there is a
giant pit called Meteor
Crater. It is nearly a mile

Meteor Crater

across and about six
hundred feet deep. It is
thought that this crater
was made by a huge
meteorite 25,000 years
ago. Such huge meteorites
hit Earth only once every
50,000 years or so. Several
other huge meteorite

craters have been found throughout the world.

No meteorite has ever done great damage to a city. There is just one proven case of a person getting hit by a meteorite.

On November 30, 1954, Ann Hodges of Sylacauga, Alabama, was napping on her couch. Suddenly there was a loud crash and something hit her. A ten-pound meteorite had smashed through her roof. Luckily, Mrs. Hodges was

Meteor flashes by the Little Dipper (Ursa Minor)

only bruised on her hand and leg.

Probably you will never see a meteorite hit the ground. But it is easy to see meteors burn up in the sky. On certain nights you can see dozens of them. When this happens

Meteor shower

it is called a meteor
shower. The most famous
meteor shower occurs on
and around August 11
each year. It's called the
Perseid meteor shower
because many of the

meteors appear in the constellation Perseus.

Meteoroids are thought to have been formed in two ways. Many of them, especially the big ones, are thought to be pieces of asteroids. The asteroids collided and their fragments were thrown into Earth's orbit. The many meteoroids in showers are thought to be bits and pieces of old comets that have fallen apart.

WHAT STRUCK SIBERIA IN 1908?

A huge space object hit Siberia, Russia, in 1908.

Early on the morning of June 30 a bright object passed through the sky. People many miles away said the object was brighter than the sun. There was a tremendous crash. Fifty miles from where the object hit, trees

Comet Ikeya-Seki photographed in 1965

were ripped away and windows were broken. Luckily, few people lived in the area. The only loss of life was a reindeer herd.

What struck Siberia that morning? No pieces of the

The Zodiacal light and comet Ikeya-Seki were
visible with the naked eye on the morning of October 26, 1965.

object were found. Many
scientists think it was a
huge meteorite. They say
that no pieces were found
because the meteorite
exploded into dust on its
way down. Others think it
was the head of a small

comet. They say that pieces weren't found because the ice melted when it struck.

A comet, asteroid, or giant meteorite would cause great damage if it struck a city. The chances of that happening are small. But because it could happen, scientists have thought up ways to avoid such collisions. One plan is to bomb the object away from Earth's orbit before it hits our planet.

Comet West photographed in 1976. Its dust trail is
white, while its gas trail appears blue.

CLUES TO THE PAST

Comets, meteors, and asteroids are lovely to look at. Scientists have another reason to study them. They learn about the history of Earth and the solar system from them.

For example, meteorites were formed when the solar system began—4.5 billion years ago. By studying the materials in meteorites, scientists learn

more about how our solar
system began.

Some scientists feel that
meteorites and other space
objects have affected life
on Earth. One theory
concerns the dinosaurs.

Starting about 225
million years ago dinosaurs
walked on Earth. About 65
million years ago they died
out. Why? Some scientists
say that a huge meteorite

or asteroid was to blame. They say that the huge object kicked up great amounts of dust when it struck Earth. The dust blocked out sunlight, causing plants to die. The dinosaurs had no food, so they died, too.

Dinosaur footprints

Another theory about meteorites is really unusual. Meteorites have been found to contain the amino acids needed by living things. Some scientists say that meteorites helped begin life on Earth by dropping those materials like seeds on our planet.

Close-up of the 82-inch telescope at McDonald Observatory

A FEW FAMOUS COMETS

Comet	When Discovered	Years Taken to Orbit Sun
Halley's Comet	Over 2,000 years ago	About 76
Encke's Comet	1786	3.3
Great Comet of 1843	1843	513
Donati's Comet	1858	2,000
Kohoutek's Comet	1973	75,000

THE FOUR LARGEST ASTEROIDS

Asteroid	Year Discovered	Diameter in Miles
Ceres	1801	485
Pallas	1802	304
Juno	1804	118
Vesta	1807	243

SOME YEARLY METEOR SHOWERS

Name	Dates	Constellations Where Many Are Seen	Number Seen per Hour in Dark Place
Quadrantids	January 1-6	In the area of Boötes and Draco	50
May Aquarids	May 1-6	Aquarius	20
Perseids	August 10-14	Perseus	50
Orionids	October 18-23	Orion	20
Leonids	November 14-18	Leo	20
Geminids	December 10-13	Gemini	50

Comet
Ikeya-Seki

You'll enjoy it if you ever see a comet, meteor, or asteroid. Remember, too, that they help teach us about the universe in which we live.

WORDS YOU SHOULD KNOW

asteroids(AST • uh • roydz)—the numerous objects, made of rock and metal, that are located between Mars and Jupiter

astronomy(ast•RON •ah •mee)—the study of stars, planets, and other heavenly bodies

comets(KAH •metz)—objects made of ice, dust, metal, gases, and rock that have long glowing tails when near the sun

constellation(KAHN •steh •LAY •shun)—a star group in a certain area of the sky

crater(CRAY •ter)—a pit in the ground made by an object such as a meteorite

diameter(dye •AM •ih •ter)—the distance of a line drawn through the center of a circle or round object

fireball(FYE •er •ball)—a very bright meteor

head (of a comet)(HED)—the part that contains a comet's most solid material

iron meteorites(EYE •urn MEE •tee •or •ites)—ones made of many kinds of metals—mainly iron and nickel

meteorites(MEE •tee •or •ites)—meteoroids that hit the ground

meteoroids(MEE •tee •or •oydz)—particles of stone or metal in the solar system

meteors(MEE •tee •orz)—meteoroids that appear as streaks of light when they burn up in Earth's atmosphere

meteor shower(MEE •tee •or)—an event that occurs when many meteors can be seen at a certain time

million(MILL •yun)—a thousand thousand (1,000,000)

moons(MOONZ)—natural objects that orbit the planets

orbit(OR •bit)—the path an object takes when it moves around another object

planets(PLAN •etz)—the nine big objects that orbit the sun

solar system(SO •ler SISS •tem)—the sun and all objects that orbit it

solar wind(SO •ler WIND)—a wind that results from expanding gases in the sun

star(STAHR) — a giant ball of hot glowing gas

stony meteorites(STOW • nee MEE • tee • or • ites) — ones made of many kinds of stones

sun(SUHN) — the star closest to Earth

tail (of a comet)(TAYLE) — the trail of dust and gases that fans out from the comet's head

telescopes(TEL • ih • skopes) — instruments that make distant objects look closer

theory(THEER • ee) — an idea, often unproven, about why something occurs

universe(YOON • nih • virss) — all of space and everything that's in it

Zodiacal light (zoh • DYE • ih • kil LITE) — a soft glow seen in the sky; in the east before sunrise, and in the west before sunset

INDEX

About the Author

Dennis Fradin attended Northwestern University on a partial creative writing scholarship and was graduated in 1967. He has published stories and articles in such places as Ingenue, The Saturday Evening Post, Scholastic, Chicago, and National Humane Review. His previous books include the Young People's Stories of Our States series for Childrens Press and Bad Luck Tony for Prentice-Hall. He is married and the father of three children.
In the New True Book series, Dennis has written about Archaeology, Astronomy, Farming, Movies, Olympics, and Skylab.